MY FIRST LOOK AT PETS

THERE ARE SNAKES ALL AROUND THE WORLD

Snakes

VALERIE BODDEN

CREATIVE EDUCATION

Published by Creative Education

P.O. Box 227, Mankato, Minnesota 56002

www.thecreativecompany.us

Creative Education is an imprint of The Creative Company

Design by Rita Marshall

Production by CG Book

Photographs by Dreamstime (Kiankhoon, Mmphotography, Rdodson, Stevebyland), Getty

Images (Michael & Patricia Fogden, Pete Oxford, Norbert Rosing, SA Team/Foto Natura)

Copyright © 2009 Creative Education

Printed in the United States of America

Library of Congress Cataloging-in-Publication Data

Bodden, Valerie. Snakes / by Valerie Bodden.

p. cm. — (My first look at pets)

ISBN 978-1-58341-724-9

I. Snakes as pets—Juvenile literature. I. Title. II. Series.

SF459.S5B63 2009   636.3'96—dc22   2007051657

First edition 9 8 7 6 5 4 3 2 1

SNAKES

SCALY SLIDERS

Snakes are different from many other kinds of pets. They do not run or jump. They do not cuddle. But pet snakes can still be fun animals to keep.

Snakes are long animals with no legs. They move across the ground by sliding. A snake's body is covered with smooth, dry scales. The scales help protect the snake.

GARTER SNAKES ARE A COMMON KIND OF SNAKE

Snakes have a **forked** tongue. Their tongue helps them pick up smells from the air. Snakes do not hear very well. But they can feel the ground **vibrate** when another animal moves. This helps them know when other animals are close to them.

Choosing a Snake

There are about 3,000 kinds of snakes in the world. Some live only in the wild. Others can be kept as pets.

Most snakes should not

be kept with other snakes

because they might fight.

Snakes come in lots of colors. Some snakes are green or brown. Others are red or yellow. Some are covered in **patterns**.

Snakes come in many sizes, too. Small snakes are usually easier to take care of than big snakes. Corn snakes and garter snakes are small snakes. These snakes are usually gentle.

Some snakes' colors help
them blend in with grass or
trees and hide from other animals.

Some snakes get very big. Burmese (*bur-MEEZ*) pythons can be much longer and heavier than a grown-up person. They can be dangerous to keep as pets. **Poisonous** snakes make dangerous pets, too.

Snake Care

Snakes need to be kept in a glass tank with a screen on top. The tank should be big enough for the snake to move around in. The floor of the tank should be covered with dirt or newspaper. There should be a heat lamp above one end of the tank.

PYTHONS ARE BIG SNAKES THAT NEED BIG TANKS

Snakes need lots of healthy food. Some snakes eat bugs or worms. Others eat mice or lizards. Snakes do not eat every day. Most eat only once a week. Snakes need fresh water, too.

If a snake gets sick, it needs to be taken to a **veterinarian**. Most pet snakes live about 10 to 15 years.

A SNAKE CAN OPEN ITS MOUTH VERY WIDE TO EAT

Snake Fun

Snakes do not like to be petted like many other animals do. But some snakes will let their owners pick them up. Two hands are needed to pick up a snake. One hand should go behind its head. The other hand should be placed around the middle of its body.

Snakes' bodies are

always the same temperature

as the air around them.

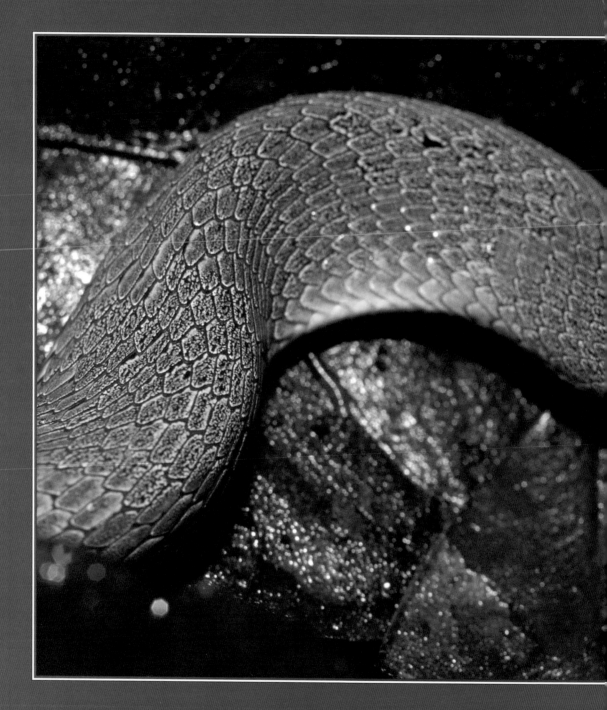

THIS SNAKE HAS BRIGHT BLUE AND YELLOW COLORING

Snakes are not playful animals. But they can still be fun to watch. Some snakes will climb up branches in their tank. Others like to lie in a bowl of water. Watching a snake helps its owner make sure it is healthy. And it shows the snake that its owner loves it!

SOME SNAKES LIKE TO REST HIGH UP IN BRANCHES

Hands-on: Seeing Vibrations

Snakes can feel the ground vibrate when other animals move across it. Use this activity to help you see how vibrations are made.

What You Need

An empty coffee can with a plastic lid
A handful of dry rice
A metal spoon

What You Do

1. Put the lid tightly on the coffee can.
2. Place the rice in the center of the lid.
3. Hold the coffee can still with one hand. With the other hand, hit the side of the coffee can with the spoon.
4. The vibrations made when the spoon hits the coffee can will make the rice jump!

WILD SNAKES USE VIBRATIONS TO HELP CATCH FOOD

Index

Words to Know

forked—split into two or more parts

patterns—designs that are repeated

poisonous—containing something that can make people sick or kill them

veterinarian—an animal doctor

vibrate—to move back and forth very fast

Read More

Gunzi, Christiane. *The Best Book of Snakes.* New York: Kingfisher, 2003.

Ling, Mary, and Mary Atkinson. *The Snake Book.* New York: Dorling Kindersley, 2000.

Thomson, Sarah. *Amazing Snakes!* New York: HarperCollins, 2006.

Explore the Web

Enchanted Learning: Snake Coloring Pages

> http://www.enchantedlearning.com/painting/snakes.shtml

Kidzone: Snakes

> http://www.kidzone.ws/lw/snakes/index.htm

Reptile Keeper: Snake Photos http://www.reptilekeeper.co.uk/
snakephotoalbum/SnakePhotos/index.html